INTO THE MYSTERY

My True Stories of Supernatural Grace

Donna Davies

INTO THE MYSTERY

My True Stories of Supernatural Grace

Watercolor Illustrations by Donna Davies

ISBN 978-0-578-87698-6

What is Supernatural Grace?

Supernatural grace is the surprising,
awe inspiring gift from the one,
loving Source and Center of all there is.

Table of Contents

Spirit Animals

In ancient times cats were worshipped as gods;
they have not forgotten this.
Terry Pratchett

On a night when my young son was staying with relatives, I was alone in our condo. Although I have lived with cats before, at the time we didn't have any pets. Our home was up a long, winding lane deep in the Connecticut woods. It was both private and quiet. But in the middle of that night, I was jolted from a deep sleep by alarming noises coming from *inside* my house. I quickly sat up in bed and held my breath, while all of my senses went on Red Alert.

The light switch was all the way across the bedroom, near the open hallway door, and to get there I would have to cross the floor in my bare feet. It was far too scary to consider as I could clearly hear an animal walking down the hall toward that same door. I sat rigid. I could guess from the sound of its heavy, waddling footfalls and belabored breathing that the animal was the size of a large raccoon or a small dog, but the sound of its movement was completely different.

My thoughts raced wildly. How in the world did an animal that big get inside? All my doors and windows were shut and locked. *Is it vicious?* I wondered. *Will it attack me? How is this even possible?* Finally, the animal reached the end of the hall and entered my bedroom. In complete darkness, I heard it pass the foot of my bed, plod along the carpet, and enter the master bath. I distinctly heard its steps on the tile and its breathing. And then, it stopped. No sound. I sat for another minute and eventually mustered the courage to scramble out of bed and flip on the light. Slowly, I moved toward the bath to investigate. Nothing was there! There wasn't an animal anywhere to be found inside the house.

What a mystery! That experience remained unsolved for so long I thought I would have to wait until I reached the *Pearly Gates* before I would learn the answer, hoping I could coax it from St. Peter himself. Rehearsing my question, I assumed it would go something like this: "St. Peter, I hate to bother you, but could you answer just one little question? What happened the night *that animal* came through my house? What was it? How did he get in? How did he get out? Why was he there? And *what was he thinking?*" Fortunately, I didn't have to wait *that* long.

In my early 30s and propelled by a marital crisis, I embarked on an intense four-year spiritual journey. During that odyssey, I was introduced to the concept of spirit animals. These animals often appear as guides and represent various traits and skills we need to learn. They can continue to appear throughout our lives, too. Call me crazy, but I wasn't going to deny an animal the chance to teach me an important lesson or two. One of my fellow seekers told me about a brilliant encounter she had with an eagle that flew directly toward her in an otherworldly face-to-face moment of sublime communication.

So I invited, and fully expected, a future rendezvous with my spirit animal. I particularly fancied the idea of meeting a rare beauty - a powerful, exotic Siberian tiger that would choose to be my guide.

In the meantime, a few months after my experience with the mysterious night visitor, I happened to be at my soon-to-be ex-husband's house. I paused alone in the thick woods behind the house we'd shared, surveying the beauty of the place, tied up so tightly in melancholy memories.

Suddenly, I heard an animal emerge in the woods and watched as it approached, waddling right toward me without hesitation. What an unusual event! It certainly caught my attention, as I had never seen an animal like it in the seven years I lived in and walked through those woods. It was very chubby and low to the ground, with very short legs. I found no reason to be afraid of him and I guess the feeling was mutual because it came right up to me before lumbering off. I recognized it from pictures I'd previously seen - it was one big, hefty groundhog.

Still, I didn't put two and two together. The angels must have been laughing over the scary night time animal visitation.

"Boy, did we frighten her! What should we try next? Something in the daylight?"

Then like peeling an onion, the riddle started to reveal itself in layers. Years later, I told the story of my nighttime visitor to an intuitive counselor who asked me if the condo was in the woods. I told her it was and that I was sure the builder had to cut down many trees. "What you experienced was a ghost animal," she delivered with conviction. Although that thought never occurred to me, it felt absolutely right.

Mulling this over, I remembered the daytime encounter with the groundhog, recognizing the same short-legged lumbering footfalls, the same size, heavy breathing and fearlessness. I surmised my night visitor had been a groundhog, too. *The groundhog chose me!* My spirit animal was a chubby little buck-toothed vegetarian, leading the life of a solitary rodent. *What did it mean?* I wondered. *What was its message? Was I hogging the earth?*

I thought about the 1993 movie *Groundhog Day,* an irreverent, delightful comedy that had blessed me with bountiful food for thought. The main character in the film is Phil Connors (played by Bill Murray) a self-centered, egotistical, hypercritical, bombastic brute with a bad attitude who repeats the same day over and over again. He does this by ending his life, day after day, when he realizes he's trapped in time. Ultimately, he grasps that he needs to make a different choice – so he becomes perfect. Phil grows into a splendid pianist, a superb ice sculptor, a modest man, and a gracious social facilitator who successfully sets aside all ego and judgment to love people unconditionally.

I decided that the screenplay was exploring the profound question, "What would you do with eternity?" Recently, I discovered that's exactly what Danny Rubin had in mind when he wrote the screenplay.

Another layer became clear when I was teaching creative writing to elementary school students. One day, I unconsciously selected the subject of the groundhog for their writing topic. In doing some research, I learned that the groundhog is one of the rare animals on earth that enter true hibernation. Their body temperature and heart rate plunges when they sleep half the year underneath the frost line in complex burrows. Their pattern of sleeping and waking seem to be an apt metaphor to our series of lives.

Of course, the groundhog is most famous for its eponymous holiday on February 2, when the animal emerges from its burrow and portends six more weeks of winter if it sees its shadow. The shadow is prominently known in psychology as the dark side of the personality, all which is repressed and unconscious. Yet another layer of the mystery is revealed in looking at the shadow. By bringing our shadow into the light, we can see how we've projected our dark thoughts and fears onto other people. Then we can forgive ourselves and begin to heal.

My good-natured groundhog may enter my life again to teach me yet another lesson. I believe the creature appeared to remind me I've done all of this before. I've lived over and over again and need to get this business of living right *this time* by choosing a loving attitude with all people in all situations and leave fear behind.

Creating the Experience

I never panic when I get lost.
I just change where it is I want to go.
Rita Rudner

As I approached the trailhead, I saw a little sign the park rangers installed, probably for student groups that read: If you are quiet, you will see wildlife. "Oh, *I* can be *very* quiet," I whispered to the sign. My adult sisters were napping in the car, too tired from our first hike in a different part of this Florida preserve to join me. But I was a woman on a mission; I was Max finding Where the Wild Things Are. I had already investigated every riverbank for alligators. Not finding one, however, did not discourage me. Instead, I moved past the little sign stepping silently into a heavily wooded path.

I had not traveled even 50 feet before an animal the size of a deer suddenly appeared and paused on the trail to look at me. In an instant, I realized it was a Florida panther, one of the most rare and endangered mammals on the planet! Breathlessly, I walked closer to him, admiring his beauty and grace before he slipped soundlessly back into the dark, dense forest.

By the time I fully expected to see wildness in that Florida preserve, I was well into my 50s and no longer a novice to creating my experiences. But when I was a younger woman, I certainly felt buffeted, often clobbered by events, relationships, and circumstances beyond my control. All that changed when I ventured on that metaphysical journey I mentioned, beginning at age 31, and learned about manifesting.

Ready to plant new seeds for my being in the world, I joined a class of spiritual seekers who, like me and Guy Noir, were eager to find the answers to life's persistent questions. There I was introduced to the concept that thoughts always precede material manifestation and that everything is a product of our thoughts. We are co-creators. I grew into the awareness that we have power to manifest our desires through focus, clarity, emotion, and trust.

To demonstrate the power of my thoughts, a classmate enthusiastically suggested I make clouds disappear. So on a lovely warm day, I flopped down on the grass and selected a puffy little cloud in the sky. I focused on sending heat to the cloud, and as I did so, the cloud quickly became smaller and smaller until it completely disappeared. I was astonished to see such fast results, and the experience left me feeling very empowered.

Then another student suggested I "become invisible" and witness the effects. I chose a busy department store and focused my thoughts again by repeating the mantra "I am invisible" while walking through the aisles. By the time I reached the check-out line, three people had run into me. What a stunning success!

I soon had an opportunity to try this out in a more practical setting when I discovered one day that my husband had forgotten his wallet. He was heading toward the airport for a three-day trip and had driven only ten minutes when I realized his billfold was still at the house. As this was long before cell phones, I said to my young son, Ryan, "We need to send Dad a message to turn around and come home to get his wallet." As we sat together, we focused on saying the message out loud several times. Ten minutes later, my husband walked into the house because "something" made him think about his wallet, look for it, and return home.

Before those first demonstrations of power, I had held onto the limiting belief that I was a victim of other people's decisions and actions. Observing the effect of my thoughts convinced me that the real power of creating life's circumstances resided within me. I also understood that I had to accept *complete responsibility* for creating my life, both the good and the bad. This also meant I had to decide what I did and didn't want in my life, so I could provide clear direction for my thoughts. Resistance set in. Did I want to be held accountable for the results? Did I *really* want to grow up? Clearly it was time to quit blaming Mom.

I soon found I could manifest more easily if I was emotionally involved in the situation. Wanting to help those I cared about most provided many opportunities to see this in action. When Ryan was going through a period of feeling very anxious, I decided to help him learn to manifest a calmer mindset. We talked about his fears, and then I took an imaginary balloon out of the air, opened a little door on the side of it, and asked Ryan to place all of his concerns inside the balloon. We opened his bedroom window, released the imaginary balloon and watched it rise in the sky until it disappeared. His anxiety sailed away along with the balloon and we were both relieved the exercise had been a success.

Later, when Ryan was dealing with flagging self-confidence, I helped him manifest more self-assurance. I made a recording and played the tape by his bedside after he fell asleep each night. The recording repeated the following script over and over: "I am completely loved, safe and secure. I am happy, healthy, strong, confident, smart, powerful and capable. I have many friends and participate in many wonderful activities. I am filled with joy." My son soon seemed to be a more confident boy.

Not long afterward, a shy friend was getting married for the second time and confessed to me that she felt deeply anxious about being the center of attention at the ceremony. We were very close and our strong bond created an equally strong desire to help her. As I sat down in the large, bright sanctuary before the well-attended service, I closed my eyes, took several deep breaths and relaxed as I focused on the bride waiting in the narthex. For several minutes, I pictured my friend in a beautiful long gown, holding her bouquet, and imagined she was enclosed in a perfect ball of golden light. Inside the ball, she was completely relaxed, filled with ease, and suffused with joy.

A few weeks after the honeymoon, we met for lunch and talked about the wedding. "The most remarkable thing happened before I walked down the aisle," my friend told me. I smiled, guessing what might come next. "I stopped being nervous and felt perfectly calm and happy."

When someone is injured or ill, fear can loom large so trusting in a loving God or Universe to manifest our good becomes essential. Before a scheduled surgery, my friend Diane envisioned a caring, dedicated, highly competent team of doctors and nurses operating on her while they listened to soothing music in a brightly lit, sparkling clean room. She relaxed, let go, and trusted in a loving Universe. Her surgery went smoothly and she recovered quickly.

Similarly, when I had an amniocentesis, I asked for a quiet two minutes before the doctor and technician began the procedure. After breathing deeply, I relaxed my muscles and mentally left my body to be in one of my favorite places. Then, I let go, and let God. In both our circumstances, our preparation of envisioning, our relaxation, and our trust made challenging medical events free from fear.

After I shared these stories with my son's fiancée, Amy, she soon had an opportunity to try the same sort of technique. She was rock climbing with a group when her friend Carin fell 15 to 20 feet and twisted her ankle when her foot hit a ledge. As Amy drove her injured companion to an urgent care center, they talked about how hard it was going to be for Carin to rest her body while her ankle healed because she was used to being very active. Carin was scared that it was going to be a bad break that might require months of recovery or even surgery.

Remembering my stories, Amy decided to speak to the Universe directly. "Carin is one of your biggest fans!" she said out loud. "Every single day, she gets outside to appreciate and bask in the bounty and wonder of your natural beauty. While we understand that she may need to rest for a week or two, we know she will be strong, healthy, and well again. Very soon, she will be ready to pursue outdoor activities that help her enjoy and explore this natural wonderland daily."

The doctors x-rayed Carin's ankle, and they were all blown away by the results. Despite Carin's description of the fall and her pain, no breaks or fissures showed on the X-ray at all. She was left with only some bruises and a light, soft-tissue sprain! The doctor recommended she rest for one to three weeks before resuming activity. Upon hearing the news, Carin looked at Amy and declared, 'The Universe provides!'"

The seeds of my being are the result of my choices. A Course in Miracles makes the idea of choosing very simple. We can either choose love or fear - the only two emotions that exist. Whenever I have made a decision out of fear, it has been the wrong one; the one that leads me away from my highest good.

Thoughts are things. Thoughts are *not nothing* and they are certainly *not neutral*. Our thoughts set up an energy pattern around us that attracts like things. If we sow pessimistic, fearful thoughts, we are commanding negative circumstances and depressing environments to grow. But if we choose love, think love, and become love, we are sowing optimistic seeds that mandate positive outcomes and thriving environments.

Behind a Thin Veil

Laughter is carbonated holiness.
Anne Lamott

Right after my Mom died, I began seeing bird feathers lying on the ground. I'd pick them up and feel connected to her as it seemed to acknowledge she was light as Spirit now; her passing felt as light as a feather in my soul. By then, I was fully aware of the continuation of life on the other side of the veil, so I was not bereft. When Ryan found coins and bills on the ground, he knew it was a message of love from Grandma who made it a habit of giving him money. Since my Dad passed, I often see yellow swallowtail butterflies and by paying attention to them, I honor his life once again. But one time, I had an experience with someone on the other side of the veil that blew me out of the water, like the time when my parasail (attached to a jetboat) did, raising me high in the sky over the Choctawhatchee Bay.

When my first husband, Dick, and I were stationed at Luke Air Force Base in Phoenix, we met a fellow pilot, Willie Mays, who became our fast friend. Dick and Willie flew training sorties in F-4 Phantom jets during the day while I worked at Goldwater's department store downtown. Most nights, Willie joined us for a home-cooked meal or treated us to dinner out. Many evenings, he and Dick repaired their old classic Corvettes in the driveway or came inside to talk.

Though we were surrounded by desert, we lived in base housing, a refreshing oasis of shade trees and lush green grass. The ambiance was heightened by the antics of my precious cat, by the equally adorable child next door, and by the heart pounding roar of F-4s taking off and landing, especially when pilots added the powerful thrust of their afterburners. The class of pilots and spouses quickly formed a festive, tight-knit social group of very young people. In fact, the flight instructors were agog at how adolescent that pilot class looked. Dick overheard one of the trainers say, "These guys are so young, especially that Mays kid. He looks like he's fourteen!"

For the three of us, those months in Arizona were a most excellent adventure. We slid down the cascading waterfalls at Oak Creek Canyon and absorbed the red rock plateaus and cliffs of Sedona. Willie and I enjoyed seeing the treasure of Navajo pottery and Hopi baskets at the Heard Museum and the paintings of the Wild West by Remington and Russell at the Phoenix Art Museum. I took them to a beautiful Scandinavian store downtown that sold my favorite home furnishings so they could admire the handsome Danish teak furniture with me.

Willie was a great storyteller, so we gradually learned he had a boat load of brothers and one sister. Every meal, they all fought over the food like a band of starving castaways, forcing his lone sister to become aggressive in order to thrive. Willie told us that after she married, it took her husband a long time to get her to slow down and be reassured there would always be plenty of food. One time, a market researcher called Willie to find out how many airlines he could name. Always the class clown, he kept her on the phone a very long time while he recited the names of thirty-five airlines he knew. But storytelling was just one of his gifts. Another was his astounding pitch perfect ability to mimic different motorcycle engines, like the distinct sounds of a Kawasaki revving up, a Harley-Davidson at full throttle, or a Suzuki powering down.

When F-4 training was over, the three of us were scattered, Dick to Thailand, Willie to Korea, and me to Minneapolis followed by Thailand. But after Willie volunteered for an extra year in Korea, he scored a series of plum assignments including an exchange program with the German Luftwaffe, and then as a Thunderbird pilot.

When Dick and I visited Willie and his bride in Germany, I was surprised to see lovely Danish teak furniture he had purchased to fill his house. After flying with the Luftwaffe, the Air Force welcomed him onto the elite Thunderbird team assigning him the role of official narrator the first year. He became a member of the six person precision aerial team the following year at age 31 flying sleek, supersonic T-38 Talon aircraft. He loved his work and couldn't believe the Air Force actually paid him to fly.

Then, on January 18, 1982, I heard on my car radio that four Thunderbird pilots crashed on the floor of the Nevada desert and I knew instantly Willie was one of them. They were practicing the Diamond Loop and the commander didn't climb high enough at the top. As typical in many aerial maneuvers, all the pilots keep their eyes fixed on the plane next to them. At the top of the Diamond Loop, the planes are upside down, then descend at over 400 mph as they aim toward the ground, pulling out just above it. But on that day it wasn't enough. It was the worst crash in Thunderbird history.

Stunned, I went through the motions of living, feeling like a shadow. I picked up my son from Carol, his caregiver, who was also a dear friend. When I told her of Willie's death, Carol said "Last night, you were in my dream and you told me your friend was in a plane crash."

Before the funeral, Dick and I joined his family at Willie's childhood home in Ripley, Tennessee. We stood in their dimly lit parlor talking, hugging, and crying. A couple of his brothers looked so much like Willie it took my breath away. Once we were at the massive church, it overflowed with mourners pressed into the pews, standing in the aisles, and crowding the doorways. At the grave site, there was a dramatic gun salute, a color guard folding the flag, and a bugler playing taps all marking the end of a life.

> *And if I go, while you're still here…*
> *Know that I live on,*
> *Vibrating to a different measure*
> *Behind a thin veil you cannot see through.*
> *You will not see me,*
> *So you must have faith.*[1]

About six months later, I was at a summer party floating on an air mattress in a swimming pool. In the midst of this peaceful time, I chose to reflect on Willie's life. After thinking about him for several minutes, I heard the sound of an F-4 flying right above me. I looked up into the cloudless sky, searching in every direction, but couldn't see a single plane, even though the astounding roar of the engine in full afterburner placed it directly overhead. Instead of growing and ebbing like the sound of a passing plane, the noise stayed irrationally steady and stationary.

In that moment, I realized it was Willie. He was communicating through this mysterious channel of clairaudience. The thin veil between us didn't just flutter gently aside; it blew away! He was entertaining me in the most audacious, extravagant way he could imagine, letting me know he was carrying on in style, thank you very much, maintaining his status, and polishing up his Class Clown trophy.

I felt like a queen.

Two years later, Willie was in four of my dreams in the space of just a few months. During that time, I read that if a person dies suddenly, it's possible for them to be confused and stuck in this earthly dimension. For that reason, I began to pray for him. Then one day while I was between waking and napping, I was given a vision. I clearly saw a heavy, black, old-fashioned metal safe surrounded by an intense, bright yellow light. I knew intuitively it was a message about Willie and from the simplicity of the vision, it was also obvious to me, he was now safe.

I wait for the time when we can soar together again
Both aware of each other.
Until then, live your life to the fullest
And when you need me,
Just whisper my name in your heart,
I will be there.[2]

[1, 2] "Ascension" by Colleen Hitchcock

Flashes of the Future

The future ain't what it used to be.
Yogi Berra

When I was six, I was a guest at the June wedding of my cherished kindergarten teacher, Miss Nichols, and her groom, Richard. After the ceremony, I danced around her billowing dress and touched the gossamer lace. The brilliant white gown contrasted strikingly against the deep greens of the Minnesota summer. Suddenly, I became aware with a complete sense of knowing that my husband's name would be Richard, too. Fifteen years later, it came to pass: I married a young man named Richard

This was the first time I intuitively knew something significant about my future. Throughout my life, I have had glimpses while awake and compelling dreams while asleep that revealed what would later unfold. These glimpses were not born out of a wish, or fervent desire, or even a best guess. They just seemed to happen.

The next time this occurred, I was a little older. During a scene in an episode of the 1950s television show *Father Knows Best,* the teenage daughter, Betty Anderson (played by Elinor Donahue), pensively watches a plane piloted by her boyfriend fly off to war and possible death. As I watched, I realized I was seeing my future. I knew intuitively I would be involved with people in the military whose lives would be at risk and I felt a similar, keen sense of melancholy over the inevitable. This came to pass in my connection to both Dick and Willie.

I received another flash forward during my senior year in high school. Our choir and drama department produced the musical *The King and I,* in which I played Tuptim, the Burmese princess-slave given to the King of Siam. One day during rehearsal, I suddenly knew I would travel to Thailand before I ever got to Europe. How exciting to know that! Seven years later, I lived in Udon Thani, Thailand and I wouldn't get to Europe for three more years.

So how is it possible to know the future? One theory is that everything is happening all at once and chronological time is just an illusion. This suggests the past, present, and future

already exist and we are not located in a single time but scattered in every time, allowing certain knowledge to flow. Another view is that everything already happened and we are choosing to watch a movie we project. Maybe when we are between incarnations, we decide what our next life will be, who we will partner with, and what lessons we will learn – and some of this information is retained.

We must not think we are victims of time, however. We chose to be in time and space, this physical dimension, in order to experience materiality. Because we know the creations of the Source encompass all possibilities and are completely unlimited, we can safely assume there are many dimensions of life. I think we were created as immortal spirits and so death is like a door we open and close to separate our lives in the material world. If we confront and eliminate our fear of death, we can enjoy the ease of knowing we have all the time in eternity to live.

During the transition from military to civilian life, I experienced another intuitive moment of knowing what lay ahead. I was standing by the mailbox, reading my husband's offer letter from American Airlines. Despite the fact it was such welcome news, I had a premonition we would move to the Northeast outside New York City and, shockingly, that area of my mental map was covered in darkness. That daunting, bleak time came to pass and it included postpartum depression that lasted three years.

One day as I was mixing up a batch of chocolate chip cookies, a blank entry slip for the Pillsbury Bake-Off spilled out of the bag of flour. The prize was so large that winning it meant I could buy a separate place to live. I decided to enter using a recipe idea that came to me right away. I stuffed crescent rolls with a spinach rice filling, laid them in a pinwheel design, and sprinkled cheese on top. After baking, they looked unbelievably scrumptious with a flaky golden crust and bubbly melted cheese.

On the day I mailed my entry, I was instantly aware that I was going to be one of the 100 finalists, even though I knew tens of thousands of people enter each year. Months later, all 100 of us were flown to San Antonio, Texas for the competition and judging. There I was, being filmed as Bob Barker interviewed me in my tiny demonstration kitchen while I sautéed garlic and onions. (I didn't win, but a woman who lived fifteen miles from me in Connecticut won the grand prize of $100,000.)

A couple of times, I actively chose to see the future. Before I knew who my second husband would be, for example, I asked intuitively to be shown who he was. The ideas came to me that he drove a truck and wore the red and black checked shirt of an outdoorsman. Both of these were true pictures.

Some incidents of precognition came to me in dreams. As I recently read over my dream journal of 35 years, I was struck by how often something I dreamed about ended up being relevant to the following day. For instance, one dream included a man I hadn't seen for a year and he showed up in my waking life the very next day. Also, several times I became aware of a newspaper headline a day or two before it would appear.

Then, on November 11, 2015, I experienced a dream so terrifying, that while still asleep, I sat up in bed screaming at the top of my lungs. As my husband shook me awake, all the details of the dream vanished. I knew there wasn't anything causing me anxiety in my waking life. But Ryan and his partner were in Paris that week, sharing an apartment with a Frenchman who lived a block and a half from the Bataclan Theater. A day and a half after my nightmare, 90 people were killed at the Bataclan by terrorists. (Ryan and his partner, thank heavens, weren't among the victims.)

One of the most curious and stunning dreams of the future was shared by a friend. In a dream, he saw a beautiful and very memorable stain glass window. Years later, he walked into a building and was astounded to see the exact, same window.

Some dreams of the future carry significant messages. I should have paid attention to the following dream I had on the day before I bought a condo.

I was still in bed when the present owner of the condo I was considering buying called to see if I'd put an offer on it. I was exceedingly groggy and could hardly talk. Then I saw a baby being washed down a concrete ramp into a river and then saw myself being swept away into the same river by a huge wave. As I realized I couldn't keep above the top of the slushy ice water, I let go and sunk beneath it. I was conscious of one small area within the water which was illuminated and it protected me, but not the baby.

Babies in dreams might represent a real baby, but usually they symbolize any kind of new venture, and in this case, it was buying a home. Water often represents emotion and certainly the wave in this dream is threatening, powerful and destructive. I wish I had realized this was a warning dream, telling me not to purchase the condo as it proved to be a terrible financial decision.

Fortunately, another dream helped push me in the right direction on another decision. When Scott, was 10, I had a dream about the two of us flying through the air over a friendly neighborhood in the country where there were many animals. I dropped Scott off to play with an affectionate black and white kitty.

Shortly after that dream, Scott's teacher strongly recommended we get a cat because she thought it would help him get through a rough patch. We went to an animal shelter to pick one out and chose one that was black and white, even though I originally preferred getting a calico. The black and white one (who Scott named Sparky) seemed to pick us!

When Ryan was 10, I had a prescient dream that seemed to be an attempt to raise my awareness of his sexual orientation to my conscious level. The dream involved being offended that some gay men were engaging in intimate behavior at a restaurant where we were eating. Then the men acted out the same intimate behavior with Ryan. Seven years later, in waking life, he came out to me.

All of these mysterious glimpses into my future felt like gifts. Even though I try to live in the present, I heartily welcome the occasional glimpses of what the future holds. After all, it's like touching the indwelling Divine.

Accidentally, Speaking

Love is much nicer to be in than an automobile accident,
a tight girdle, a higher tax bracket
or a holding pattern over Philadelphia.
Judith Viorst

It was a dark and windy night when the accident happened. My first husband and I were living near Columbus Air Force Base, in Mississippi, far from our families. In that first year of our marriage, we bumbled about like two birthday party guests turning round and round, trying to pin the tail on the donkey. My Mom knew we were floundering so I decided to follow her advice and take time to smell the roses by planning a night out on the town.

Before we moved to the South, I bought my husband a classic car he had set his heart on with the $2,500 I had left over after college. It was a sweet little 1963 Chevy Corvette Stingray split window coupe that rode low to the ground. Shock absorbers must have been optional equipment. However, in its favor, the car was super stylish and painted a dazzling shade of bronze.

The summer before the accident, we were driving the 'Vette at night on a narrow, unlit, hilly, two-lane rural Mississippi highway when my husband made an impulsive decision to pass a veritable *wall* of three long tractor trailers. I was simply aghast. He sped up and was just roaring past the second long-hauler when a car came over the hill, bearing down on us. If I could have blown the canopy and ejected, I would have absolutely pulled the lever. He squeezed into the tiny space behind the lead semi at the very last possible second. While I cried, I seriously considered leaving him to save my life.

So now it was winter and here we were again on another two-lane country highway in Mississippi, unlit, narrow, winding, and nearly deserted. Our dinner in Starkville had been mediocre at best and the movie an exceedingly disturbing choice. My nervousness watching Steve McQueen and Ali MacGraw in *The Getaway* grew into dread on the drive home.

As we approached a curve and climbed a rise, I saw the headlights of a car stopped at an intersection. I intuitively knew the driver was going to pull out in front of us, but I kept quiet, too afraid of being harshly scolded for being a backseat driver.

As we reached the intersection, just as I feared, the driver pulled out onto the highway. He couldn't have timed it better for a full-on impact. I screamed and we hit him broadside while the car behind us screeched to a desperate stop. The front of our fiberglass car shattered, and the steering wheel shaft broke off and struck my husband in the chest. Surprisingly, we could all walk and function but I suffered post-traumatic stress disorder for several months after the accident, and it took all the money we saved that year to repair the car.

Years later, I heard someone declare "There are no accidents." At first, I didn't believe it but I respected the person who made the claim so I decided to test the statement for truth. In replaying the details of our crash, I realized we weren't random victims of an exceedingly inept driver. Instead, my husband and I held thought patterns that set the event in motion.

Leading up to the crash, we were both overly anxious about many things. I anguished about my relationship failures, and my husband worried about money and measuring up in pilot training, - so much so that we drew fear-based experiences to us. In addition, I was intimidated by my husband's rebukes, and in my silence and sense of powerlessness, I waived the best chance we had of avoiding the crash.

Once I unpacked that accident and realized my responsibility for it, I decided to revisit a more severe experience I had, to retest the "no accidents" idea. When I was 4 or 5 years old, I was playing in my sandbox with a friend making mud pies. She thought it would be splendid to add sawdust to them. It meant we'd have to go into the new split-level house my father was building next door, which I knew was expressly forbidden. Mom said children couldn't go into the house because there weren't any stairs yet, only a board connecting the threshold of the front door to the upper floor. Obeying her was part of being the good little girl that I was.

However, my playmate was very strong willed, - one tough cookie - and her arguments must have been pretty persuasive. I was also fully aware of my own sure-footed coordination, so we scurried off on our mischievous mission. We dashed up the plank and into the bedrooms of the new house, where we loaded up our little pails with fresh, light sawdust. I finished collecting mine and raced back to the top of the board first because I was afraid Mom would discover us. After making a step onto the solid board, I inexplicably blanked out and stepped off into thin air, falling eight feet to the cement floor below.

A workman in the basement picked me up and carried me next door to my horrified mother. I was unconscious for many hours. X-rays revealed I had a fractured skull, brain concussion, and a broken collarbone. It took more than half a year for my body to heal.

In analyzing that experience, I determined it wasn't an accident either. Knowing I was disobeying Mom, I felt tremendously guilty, ashamed, and sinful. If my pal and I had returned to the sandbox unhurt and Mom found out about our mischief, I don't know how she or my dad would have disciplined me. However, they never got the chance because *I punished myself!*

At 4 years old, I was not a car crash waiting to happen. I was a sweet little girl with sweet little thoughts who cooked up a devastating experience in the time it takes to soft boil an egg. Suddenly, I realized guilt is not a neutral, harmless emotion in which one can safely indulge. Guilt is so potentially dangerous that it can be fatal.

Once I was aware of this, I became very careful not to make rules for the son I was still raising, rules he might not be able or willing to obey. I didn't want to create guilt traps and have him reap any dire consequences like I did.

That morning making mud pies, the still small voice within me was actually pretty strident, the one I refused to follow with all my might. And I heard the strong voice within me the evening of the car crash, too, and resisted it energetically. As evidenced by my "accidents," thinking fearful thoughts is truly treacherous to a person's emotional, mental, and physical well being.

Naming our fear, fully unmasking it, begins the process of becoming aware of our feelings and changing them. By facing the fearful idea, we can approach even the smallest sense of grievance, annoyance, subtle anxiety, guilt, worry, conflict or failure - with curiosity and ask ourselves, *What am I afraid of?* If we ask at a quiet time and then listen, we can intuitively hear Spirit. This helps us identify the mistaken belief. Then we can ask to be shown the truth and the most helpful way forward out of the concerning situation.

Intuition grows with practice, so years ago, I decided to encourage listening to the voice of Spirit by writing down what I heard in a small notebook I keep in a handy location. In reading through my day journal, I see that I have sensed *many* reminders that seemed to arise from guidance within me. For example, I was alerted to the fact that I left my backpack in an airport lounge, so I ran back to get it in time. Spirit whispered to me that I left my watch in the school kitchen, so I retrieved it safely. Spirit's voice led me to see my glasses on the floor of the airplane so I didn't step on them or leave them behind. Similarly, Spirit has often led me to find friends' missing passports, signed documents, lost gifts, or important files.

Many entries in the journal also remind me of times when listening to Spirit's voice exceeded simple reminders and finding material things. Some examples include when Spirit made me aware of an opportunity to teach music that enriched my life. Later on, Spirit directed me to the answer for managing my class of elementary students. Spirit also urged me to embrace a friend who was trying to be invisible which led to the healing of our relationship.

By paying attention to our grievances and being open to Spirit's voice more often, I find nothing is too small or too large to benefit from the inspiration Spirit delivers. These ideas show up as an urge, a feeling, or a thought, and by acting on the message instead of ignoring or resisting it, I open myself up to miracles, right actions, and a more serene path.

Entangled

What if everything is an illusion and nothing exists?
In that case, I definitely overpaid for my carpet.
Woody Allen

Just as certain truths are revealed and relationships are made whole by an attitude of reverence or wonder, so is science informed by the same approach. As Colin Tudge wrote in *The Tree* (Crown, 2005), "Pythagoras, five centuries before Christ, saw science (as he then construed it) as a Divine pursuit. Galileo, Newton, Ray, and the rest saw their researches as a form of reverence." Keeping an open mind and an outlook touched by wonder enables scientists to discover truths about life. The astounding discovery of entanglement is just one example.

Quantum entanglement is measurable on the subatomic level. When scientists do something to one half of a subatomic particle that has been split in two, the other half is affected, no matter how far away it happens to be. Einstein called this entanglement "spooky action at a distance."

Scientists have further proven that the location of subatomic particles is dependent on observation. Until someone gives it attention, a single particle can reside in different locations at the same time. Yet the act of observing a particle in one of those places collapses all the other locations into that one. No one knows why. It's as if when we consider one position, the particle decides to be in that one place because it's entangled with us.

Until recently, this "spooky action" appeared to be information that is instantly known—teleported or transferred with no visible, physical substance. But with the discovery of the Higgs boson particle (nicknamed the "God particle"), our understanding has changed somewhat. The Higgs boson carries the mass property information and shares it with other particles, even ones that are separated from one another in space. Although it is not yet proven, some scientists believe every particle in the Universe is entangled with every other one.

"We all dance to a mysterious tune," Einstein said, "and the piper who plays this melody from an inscrutable distance—whatever name we give him—Creative Force, or God—escapes all book knowledge." Quantum physicists are very close to suggesting what many of us have believed for quite some time—that on a subnuclear level, we are all one and that we create our own reality from a perpetual potpourri of possibilities.

Are these particles or atoms truly physical matter to begin with? Good question! Classic studies in quantum physics demonstrate that electrons initially act like waves (energetic frequencies that have no mass) and pass through several openings in an obstacle and meet again on the other side. But oddly enough, that only happens when no one is observing the electron. When scientists put their attention on the electron, it instead acts like a particle (physical matter), not a wave. It then goes through only one opening, not all of them.

Perhaps then matter is insubstantial, composed of intentions, desires, and ideas—in other words, energy instead of mass. William Blake could have been suggesting this possibility when he wrote these famous lines: "To see a world in a grain of sand/ And a heaven in a wild flower/ Hold infinity in the palm of your hand/ And eternity in an hour."

When I was about 7-years- old, something happened that revealed this concept to me in a once-in-a-lifetime event. My father and I were sitting in the car in the driveway on a lovely, sunny day, having just returned from an errand. In an instant, a breach seemed to occur in the Universe, but only to me. A figurative scrim fell apart before me in kaleidoscopic waves, and I saw with complete truth and certainty that the car, the house in front of me, and the whole world around me were not real.

I was simply astonished, aghast. If it had happened to me when I was an adult, I would have said out loud: "What's going on? Hey, mission control! Did someone spill coffee on their keyboard? There's been a glitch here! Someone please fix it!"

But back then, I was Dorothy skipping on the Yellow Brick Road discovering that the Wizard of Oz was a fake. I was Jim Carrey in *The Truman Show* learning I had been oblivious to the fact that my family was simply acting out their roles in a reality TV show since my birth. What a stunning thing to happen to a child! And what in the world is a 7-year-old to do with this knowledge?

Decades later, I was introduced to holography when I saw the captivating crystal ball in the Haunted Mansion at Disney World. This prop plays host to a precise three-dimensional image of a woman's face. When the attraction first opened, as the cars on the track circled the ball, riders could see and hear her talking and moving her head from all sides. It was highly engrossing.

The fascinating principle behind holography is the idea that the boundary around a certain space contains all the information about what's inside. Even just a fragment of the original still contains the whole picture. If you cut a true hologram in half, for example, each half contains the whole view of the holographic image.

Years later, as I watched *Star Trek: The Next Generation*, I became familiar with the concept of holodecks—fictional virtual reality systems projected in an empty room. Like holograms, the people and scenery in the holodecks appear completely real. Within this graphic simulation of any desired reality, a person can materialize objects or make them disappear at will. While holodecks are fantasy, I know from my experience at age 7 that physical reality is not necessarily what it appears to be. Just for fun, I occasionally thank my favorite people for joining me on my holodeck!

Like me, physicist William Tiller, Ph.D., professor emeritus of the Department of Materials Science and Engineering at Stanford University, thinks the Universe is like a holodeck. "We've created it as a vehicle of experience, and we've created the laws that govern it," he told Michael Talbot in *The Holographic Universe* (Harper Collins, 1991). "And when we get to the frontiers of our understanding, we can in fact shift the laws so that we're also creating the physics as we go along."

When I became a student of *A Course in Miracles*, I was reintroduced to the idea that the world is just an illusion. Slowly, my childhood experience began to make sense. If the Universe isn't real, then time and space don't exist. Living from this perspective, a person can truly become fearless, relaxed, and accepting of everything that appears to happen here. We can practice non-attachment.

Shakespeare wrote, "Life is but a dream, within a dream." Many spiritual teachers admonish us to be *in* the world but not *of* the world. This level of disengagement makes me feel more free—lighter, and quicker to laugh, love, and enjoy life. More importantly, I am able to forgive more quickly, which seems to be a primary lesson in this school house we call earth.

On Wings of Freedom

"I tried to contain myself... but I escaped!"
Gary Paulsen

There was an invasion of gypsy moths in Connecticut in 1981, just as the forests turned summer green. A legion of caterpillars ate most of the leaves, like a biblical plague of voracious locusts devouring fields of grain. But nowhere were trees stripped barer than right around the house where my husband and I lived. Knowing that like attracts like, I thought the neighbors would intuit that the ruin outside was a reflection of the precarious relationship inside. How embarrassing!

We're all meant to grow, thrive, and live free so that in our best moments we can be creative and kind. But when growth is restrained, right creation is inhibited; the life we desire slips out of reach. We might feel constrained by partners, parents, or children, and feel vulnerable, inadequate, and unworthy. These are all obstacles to peace, being awake, and experiencing joy.

I found lots of reasons to stay in the marriage. I couldn't, as yet, imagine leaving my little boy in the care of others while working. My parents would label me a failure because divorce was antithetical to their religious beliefs. Separation seemed so shameful among my acquaintances with stable marriages. Was I independent and strong enough to be on my own? But the one question that haunted me the most was *where would I go*? One by one, I piled these bricks of fearful thoughts up high until I'd built a prison cell. I certainly didn't want to stay there. And then one night, I had this dream.

It is night and I am flying over my beloved childhood home in Minnesota, the house where my parents still live. I see vibrant, large orange poppies in the area around the house. The sky is completely dark as there isn't a moon in the sky and I don't see stars. But in spite of this, I can clearly see the poppies as if they are lit from within. I look down upon the house as I circle it, flying over the fields in the back, too, and see the neighbors' yards to either side. I feel comforted to be at my home and delighted to move so freely in the sky.

I like to think Spirit knew I needed to experience freedom again, to be reminded of how it felt, just like it did during my childhood where I never had to work for strength, opportunity, and success. Even though I was flying like a bird, I wasn't surprised as it seemed to be the most natural thing in the world. The dream was a visual delight, too, of luminescent flowers that reminded me of a Georgia O'Keeffe painting. I believe they were California poppies, answering my question '*where would I go.*'

America's renown psychic healer, Edgar Cayce, wrote "there is a Center in the Universe where each person, each creature and creation was known and helped constantly from this Center. He likened it to a bright light and each person was on the end of a ray extending from this ball of light. In this image, we are all one, but God the Creator is at the Center." (Edgar Cayce on Dreams, H. Bro, PhD, Warner Books). Like Cayce, I think we are inseparable from divinity and are an extension of His love. Is it possible, however, that this description is not just an image but the real deal? I think we are on the end of a ray from the *ball of light* which is the One power and Source. Some people like author, Gary R. Renard, have even been fortunate enough to see the Great Rays. (Disappearance of the Universe, Fearless Books)

About five o'clock on Christmas morning in 1983, I was lying in bed with my eyes still closed. Only my son and I were home. I wasn't fully awake yet but slowly becoming aware of how peaceful it was on that holiday morning. Then all of a sudden, I was transported to a completely different world. And, I was no longer in a human body.

I was flying in a mountain range with a deep valley that was so monumental I knew I was no longer on earth. Soaring over the trees, I flew down into the valley at breathtaking speeds with ease. My ability to see was not human for I could clearly see every leaf on every twig on every branch of every tree and all the mountains were covered with healthy green trees. Like a telephoto lens, I could zoom in on objects at a great distance by sheer intention to get a closer look. Visually searching far below me in the valley, I discovered an embankment of stone probably built by people, although I didn't see anyone. It appeared to be a fountain. Lush green, abundant plants cascaded down this embankment. My sight zoomed out again while I flew for several more seconds. Then, the vision faded and I remained lying in bed, astonished.

That morning, I received a Christmas gift which was the most momentous thing of my whole life. In that revelation, I experienced my *Self as Spirit* with the capacities of flight, complete holistic sight, total freedom, all encompassing joy, and the finest lightness of being. I was instantly in a different world, flying within a vast, sweeping environment that was just as real as the one I occupied in bed. From that day on, I have lived with an unshakable faith in the loving and powerful Source of all that is.

The idea that we are "*known and helped constantly from this Center*" was impressed upon me once again when I was only months away from separating and moving out of the house. The stress of that time weighed heavily on me when I had this dream.

> *A hot air balloon with a gondola appeared on the ground in front of me. The balloon was completely covered with beautiful, luscious, deep purple roses. There was just enough room in the gondola for one person, for me. I stepped inside the basket and ascended to the sky.*

My favorite flowers are roses so I was dazzled that they covered every inch of the balloon with their fresh, natural beauty. I've never encountered deep purple roses so I revered their uniqueness and their symbolism of divinity. During my meditation the following morning, I asked Spirit to guide me in understanding the dream. So, I wrote down the question, "What does this image mean?" Then, setting aside my conscious mind, I wrote down the two sentences I received. The answer flowed quickly without effort, so I knew I was hearing correctly. "This dream is from the spiritual world. We knew you needed to be uplifted."

By the time I rode in that dream balloon, I had taken steps to take charge of my life, change my thinking and dismantle the bricks of my cell. I meditated each day, read lots of helpful books including ones on assertiveness and others on developing a positive, optimistic attitude. To breathe more deeply for meditation, I took up running, and to have much more energy, I stopped eating almost all sugar. I dismissed the concept of sin, recognizing instead that we make *mistakes*. Importantly, my consciousness grew to know each person is equally worthy, valuable, and important.

When Ryan was seven, we moved to a nearby town. I found a career in which I thrived and we lived there for several years. Later, my high school sweetheart and I became reacquainted and were married near our families in Minneapolis. Three months into my new marriage, living in California, the expansiveness I felt was very evident in this dream.

I am in a beautiful, massive palace and need to get to another part of it quickly, so I begin flying. As I pass over the mirrored floor, I see the image of a diamond which is crystal clear, sparkling and turning around and around. I smile when I realize it is the reflection of a chandelier above me.

I marvelled at the sparkling light throughout the luxurious palace bouncing off the mirrored floor. Because of the vast scale, flying was the best way to travel quickly through all of it. Diamonds symbolize marriage and fidelity and the chandelier was a giant ball of light, perhaps a symbol of the Center. Here is the second half of that dream.

> *It is a winter night in Minnesota and there is a circle of terracotta sculptures, human figures, suspended in the air. As I swoop gracefully up and fly around them, I become lucid; my conscious mind is completely aware. Now as I study the face of one, a gentle woman, she turns her head to follow my flight and smiles at me. Stunned and elated, I smile back.*

I was deeply touched when the statue became animated and connected with me. She reminded me of a terracotta sculpture my father, a professional artist, made of my head when I was a young teen. Years later, as I watched HBO's preeminent "*Angels in America,*" the camera glides slowly down to get close to a tall angel statue in Central Park when all of a sudden, the angel lifts her head and looks directly at us, the audience. The synchronicity took my breath away.

In order to fulfill our purpose of being creative and kind, we need to be free. In my vision and dreams, I experienced freedom by defying gravity. I flew through a vast palace, and swiftly over, around, and through an immense valley in another world. I felt the light of a shimmering chandelier and the weightlessness of a bird. With the supernatural grace from the Center, I was given the gift of being uplifted in an exquisite balloon, came face to face with a sculpture come alive, and witnessed luminescent, prescient poppies in the comfortable embrace of my childhood home. With assistance from the Source, we are never alone and always loved unconditionally.

Sacred Serpent

"The road to enlightenment is long and difficult,
and you should try not to forget snacks and magazines."
Anne Lamott

For years, I thought snakes were frightening. It began when harmless garter snakes would sometimes startle me silly as I played in the grass as a child and then Hollywood dialed up the trauma considerably. Who can forget Moses turning his shepherd's staff into a wicked, undulating cobra in *The Ten Commandments* or Indiana Jones casting light on hundreds of writhing, poisonous asps in *Raiders of the Lost Art*?

Not surprisingly, my dreams of serpents were super scary. In the three snake dreams I recorded throughout the decades, the presence of snakes mirrored very specific flavors of fear, such as the guilt, anxiety, or anger. At other times, my journal notes that I consumed too much sugar, or alcohol, or was bedeviled by PMS.

But more recently, I had an amazing and wondrous snake experience. Upon awakening around midnight one night, I was given a *vision* of a serpent winding upward, its distinct decorative scales forming a multicolored design. The intricate, unique repeating pattern in vibrant colors was breathtaking. Staring at it in my mind's eye, I was filled with awe.

I felt the vision was an encouraging blessing, but I guessed that it probably held deeper meaning. The next morning, I wrote down each one of my questions and listened within for the answer. I ended up journaling that the snake was my ego and that it would bite me. The vision was appearing now to cleanse me of all remnants of ego. The image was especially elaborate just to catch my attention. Spirit defined the ego as my self-image, the human self with all its petty concerns and judgments, and the message was to let go of my selfish needs, vanities and fears. I think it also meant for me to let go of the concept of a *separate self*, as we all share One Mind.

Unity cofounder Charles Fillmore refers to personality as the *adverse ego*, a false self that is responsible for our trouble. It occurs when we become attached to *sense consciousness* (the state of believing in and acting from our five physical senses, which Fillmore described as "the serpent consciousness, deluded with sensation"). "Its selfishness and greed make men grovel in the mire of materiality, when they might soar in the heavens of spirituality," Fillmore says of the adverse ego in *The Revealing Word*. (Unity Books, 1959)

He continues this lesson by using Paul's statement "I die daily." Fillmore further explained *Christian Healing* (Unity Books, 1909) that "The "I" that dies daily is personal consciousness, formed of fear, ignorance, disease, and lust for material possessions, pride, anger, and the legion of demons that cluster about the personal ego." The only savior from such a sorry state, he continues, is the Christ spirit - the spiritual ego, the superconsciousness. Only in giving ourselves wholly to this higher consciousness by constantly denying "the demands of the personal self," Fillmore instructs, can we awaken and "grow into the Divine image."

In Hinduism, the serpent symbolizes Kundalini Shakti energy, which seeks to purify and is an agent of transformation and enlightenment. It is the power of the inner Divine that rises up through the body's seven chakras (or energy centers). When each chakra is touched by the rising Divine life force, each gland begins to vibrate at a higher level. Through repeated practice, this can change the body's chemistry, causing it to become increasingly radiant or transfigured (which is the way Jesus was described).

Many years before I had the vision of the serpent, I learned about a ceremony known to accelerate a person's spiritual growth called *shaktipat,* which means "descent of grace." This ritual includes the action of transmitting spiritual energy from one person to another. A woman from India who is considered a saint transferred some of her higher spiritual energy to me and fellow pilgrims. In one part of the ceremony, she held the head of a red rose in her hands for a while and then placed it in our open hands. The flower *literally vibrated* in the palm of my hand! As we knelt, she placed her index finger on our foreheads at the position of the third eye. One by one, we fell backward to the floor because her transfer of energy was so powerful. I suddenly experienced being in the darkness of the Universe, way out in space among the tiny lights of a million stars, feeling completely free and at peace.

Shaktipat seems similar to mystic traditions in other religions. In Christianity, for instance, baptism or confirmation can be the practice that invites the energy of Spirit to enter, awaken, and enlighten a person. In the baptism of Jesus, the Spirit of God descended upon Him in the form of a dove. In John 20:22, Jesus appeared to his disciples after the resurrection and "breathed on them and said 'Receive the Holy Spirit.'" In the Jewish tradition, *shaktipat* may be analogous to the event in Deuteronomy 34:9 which says "Joshua son of Nun was full of the spirit of wisdom, for Moses had laid his hands on him." The term *shaktipat* in Kabbalah, Jewish mysticism, is *s'micha m'shefa* or *haniha*.

After having the vision of the serpent, I've been compelled to meditate often to enhance my spiritual growth and physical healing in a practical way by using color. I've selected objects from my memory with especially vivid colors: my orange pom-poms from high school, some yellow Easter eggs, a royal blue stained glass window, and the deep purple violet on my windowsill. Once I am relaxed and ready, I imagine Spirit rising from the base of my spine and pausing at each chakra. To illustrate specifically, I imagine a perfect red rose in brilliant light so I can see and *sense the vibration of red* in the area of the reproductive organs (first chakra) and so forth. The adrenals and kidneys (second chakra) are associated with orange, the pancreas (third chakra) with yellow, the heart (fourth chakra).

with green, the thyroid around the throat (fifth chakra) with blue, the pituitary at the third eye (sixth chakra) with violet and the pineal at the crown of the head (seventh chakra) with white.

In his book, *The Sun and the Shadow*, Ken Kelzer (A.R.E. Press, 1987) writes that the recipient of rising Kundalini would experience shifts in his thinking and ways of seeing the world which was true for me. Like Ken, I found my intuition was stronger and my perception became clearer. Similarly, we both became more intolerant of negative expressions from people. We realized there were no inanimate objects, that everything was alive. In addition, we were hypersensitive to people's emotions, felt jolts of energy which physically shook us, and felt reborn.

My most recent experience with a snake was quite different from my earlier ones. I was hiking with my sons in a slightly wild place where we live when we spotted a big, healthy rattlesnake moving away from the path we were on to the safety of the grass. I was grateful to see it and very thankful for the *vision* of the rising serpent, because she reminds me to deny the ego and embrace a higher consciousness.

Awestruck

When my kids become wild and unruly,
I use a nice, safe playpen. When they're finished, I climb out.
Erma Bombeck

While Scott was a student at the Waldorf School, his teacher had a uncommon way of teaching science. Like most, she carefully prepared a lesson, gathered the students around her lab table, and encouraged them to observe the experiment. But unlike others, she stretched out the time for them to marvel at what happened by refraining from explaining the science behind the demonstration that day. Instead, she let the kids live with the wonder of what they saw overnight. They had a chance to think about why the chemicals reacted the way they did, or what prompted the biological transformation, or caused the magnetic attraction. The following day, she discussed all the reasons why with her budding scientists.

I was once assigned to represent a preschool boy named Joseph in court as his Child Advocate and saw him weekly to assess his living situation. When we were outside one day, I lifted him on my lap and put a blank sheet of paper in front of him on a clipboard. Knowing how much he loved dinosaurs, I said "There's a brontosaurus hiding on this sheet of paper!" Beginning to draw, I said "Here is his really long tail. And here is his long, long neck and small head." As more and more of the animal appeared, Joseph never took his eyes off the sheet of paper. He was speechless. In fact, he paid such close attention I had time to add a leafy tree so the monstrous mammal could eat. Joseph was in awe. His curiosity and wonder sizzled like drops of water dancing in a hot frying pan. He fell in love with drawing that day and continued to illustrate in the months and years ahead.

My own preschooler, Scott, sang with me almost every day. He was showing so much interest in music I decided to prepare a piano lesson for him. At my invitation, he followed me to my piano. On that very first day, Scott fell in love with the piano. Every day for a year and a half, Scott went to the piano, twice a day, for 45 minutes each time. I would follow him and although I never called them lessons, that's what they were. We called it *playing*. In a few months, he was sight reading and using both hands, playing four notes simultaneously. When he wrote his own music, I captured it on manuscript paper so he understood he could compose music, too, and play those tunes over again.

Scott paid very close attention, just like Joseph when we were drawing, and just like the students in science class. There was potent curiosity, a sense of unlimited possibility, and the quality of something being brand new. When someone is so engrossed, it can feel like time doesn't exist. Everyone can choose to slow down and pay attention. Decades ago, this was called *living deliberately* and now it's called *mindfulness*. I know that traveling to new places inspires me to see with curiosity, wonder and a presence born of limitless possibilities. The new sights, smells and activities tend to keep me anchored in the present moment and easily inspire awe. But we don't have to leave home to experience wonder.

One day as I got out of the car in my driveway, I was surprised to see an insect resting on the roof which matched the color of my car exactly, a shiny, rich, metallic bronze. The bug appeared to have a shield of shiny armor on its back. Even when I moved closer, it stayed in place so I decided to observe it using a new spiritual practice I had just heard about. I would observe the bug intently, without bias, and filled with love in order for it to *reveal its truth.* So, I admired him, holding an attitude of wonder and love in my mind. After a couple of minutes, the bug literally revealed himself to me. He spread his armored plates, which were actually two wings folded on his back, uncovering a brilliant red body underneath and flew away.

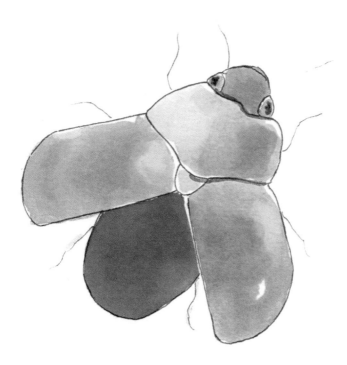

Right after that, I made lunch, grabbed a placemat, and brought it to an outdoor table. A dragonfly landed on my placemat and made himself at home. What good fortune! I could practice my special observation again. Without bias and filled with devotion which I directed to the dragonfly, I studied the exquisite black lines interlacing the turquoise green and aqua blue of her body which matched the colors of my hand woven placemat exactly. I watched the dragonfly with reverence and was rewarded with a couple more minutes of her time.

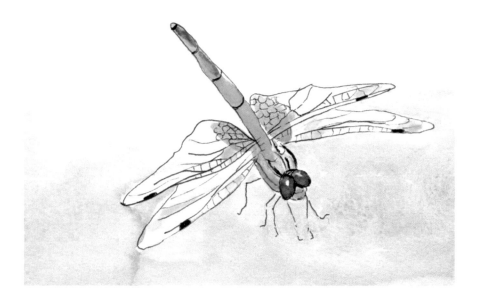

Only twenty minutes later, as I walked to my car, I was stopped by a quiet little buzzing sound. There on the garage door was a beautiful yellow bug unlike any I had seen before. I paused to admire this small creature, send it love, feeling amazed and grateful for this series of surprises from nature and the communion I felt with all three. It made me think anything can happen in this Universe and usually does when you pay attention with reverence. On that day, I confirmed what I read in *Expecting Adam*, a book by Martha Beck that "Love is the only thing on this earth that lets us see each other with the remotest accuracy." (Berkeley Books, New York, 2000)

Conversely, the attitude that seems to defeat a sense of wonder the most is judgment. Being a judge is a very weighty responsibility. It's much easier, more relaxing and lighter to choose acceptance, especially if you are motivated to make your life more sacred. Rudolf Steiner wrote in *How to Know Higher Worlds* "…just as surely as every feeling of devotion and reverence nurtures the soul's powers for higher knowledge, so every act of criticism and judgment drives these powers away." (Anthroposophic Press, Hudson, NY, 1994) My father agreed and often declared to our little family, "All criticism is destructive." It's true! Finding fault with someone or something can become a habit and perpetuates a very disturbing cycle of conflict and misery. Finding fault with someone throws away all the keys to a successful relationship.

I can attest to the power of acceptance. The motivation I found within Steiner's statement, to 'nurture the soul's powers for higher knowledge' catalyzed me into action. I selected the most challenging relationship I had and made the decision to accept that person just as they were. That day, I released my desire to change them, let go of all my criticisms, bolstered my capacity to revere and respect them, and extended my unconditional love. It was a conscious and determined thought reversal. What happened next could not have surprised me more. Our relationship pivoted one hundred and eighty degrees and was utterly healed.

Beyond acceptance, there are other attitudes and tools that predispose a person to a sense of wonder and awe. One is being kind, kind to yourself, to animals, to plants, and to all creation. Another one is thinking positive, optimistic thoughts and eliminating as many sources of negativity as possible. We can recall a fun childhood memory and share it with a friend or listen to exquisite music or the voice of a loved one. We can arrange flowers to kindle our wonder by a fragrance. By going outside, we can feel a fresh, gentle breeze, the warmth of the sun, or surround ourselves with the green of a forest or park.

Eating delicious, beautiful food or studying a piece of artwork are excellent ways to spark joy, too. Recently, I rediscovered a photo I took at the art Museo del Oro in Bogota of a face ornament representing the body of a jaguar. It was hand crafted at least seven centuries ago out of gold, carefully hand hammered and embossed. Creating or looking at a beautiful painting or ornament has the power to captivate and transport me, like the very first time I held hands with a certain young man.

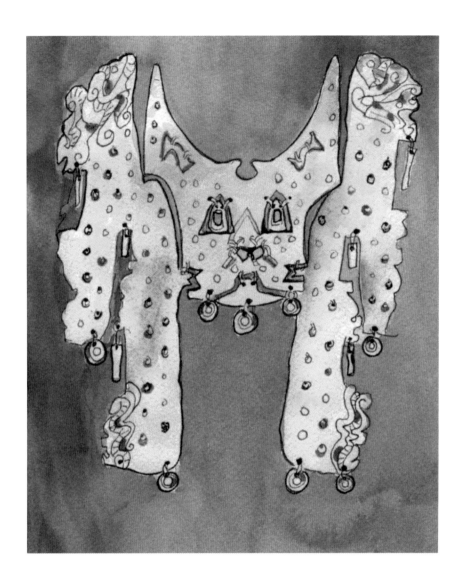

During a vacation in Minnesota, a little group of us jumped in a lake and began throwing a ball to each other. It was probably the first time I played with adults in years. For way over an hour, we bobbed in the water like kids, splashing, laughing, yelling, breathing deeply, swimming, and pretending to compete. Being playful is definitely an attitude that invites wonder.

A study on play in nature carried out by researchers at UC Berkeley in 2018 discovered that feeling awe elevates one's sense of well-being. Inviting veterans with PSTD and at risk young people from low income communities, the scholars took them on multi-day rafting trips. Now, I have to hand it to those scientists. If I designed a study, I would *definitely* include rafting trips. Or ziplining. Or parasailing. They made use of interviews, onboard cameras to record emotions, daily surveys, participant journals, and tests for stress hormones and markers of immune functions before, during and a week after each trip.

They found a 30% drop in PSTD symptoms and retention of well being almost as high among the at-risk youth. Interestingly, the awe didn't develop while running the rapids. Those moments felt both scary and thrilling. It was the time while floating in calm water between rapids that induced awe among the participants. The Berkeley team was able to predict whether a person's well being was advanced from the rafting trip from one thing and that was awe. (Yasmin Anwar, news.berkeley.edu, July 12, 2019)

In cultivating an attitude of acceptance, playfulness, and curiosity, we set ourselves up to increase our occasions of wonder. If we pay attention, or sense unlimited possibility, we can awaken reverence and marvel at the mystery around us. Admiration and love can reveal the beauty and truth of what we observe and just might cause us to become awestruck.

The Healing Art of Breathwork

Just when I discovered the meaning of life,
they changed it.
George Carlin

When I was three or four, Mom completely surprised me one day by spanking me. I don't remember what I did to aggravate her, but I was shocked by her swift swat! How dare she? How appalling! Fueled by my indignation, I drew in my breath and held it, then held it some more until I fell onto the floor, hit the corner of a toy block, and cut my cheek open. After watching her daughter get three stitches, my mother never spanked me again.

Once we leave the womb, breath is essential to life in this body. Breaths can be deep or shallow, fast or slow. For example, some people hold their breath when they are frightened while others hyperventilate. When purposefully slowing down the breath, a person can become calm or by taking deep breaths and setting an intention, one can become focused in the present. Speeded up, the breath can build energy that's needed for action or decision making. Lamaze teaches expectant mothers to control each breath during delivery in order to direct their attention away from pain and relax their muscles. Medical technicians sometimes use a pulse oximeter to measure oxygen saturation in the blood just to see how well a patient is breathing. We've all read that high intensity exercise delivers fresh oxygen to the cellular level which might slow or reverse aging. During meditation, people focus on their breathing to shift to a different level of awareness.

In Michael Talbot's enlightening book *The Holographic Universe,* I was introduced to a spiritual path that uses deep, fast breathing to take people to an alternate state of consciousness. Intrigued, I searched for more details on the website of Dr. Stanislav and Christina Grof, the founders of the healing circles called Holotropic Breathwork. They were looking for a safe way to achieve profound spiritual experiences for healing so they pioneered a practice where participants breathe deeply and quickly for three hours in a darkened setting filled with very loud, specific, evocative music. People work in pairs and take turns sitting watchfully over their partner while the whole group is led by a trained facilitator.

The Grofs used the word holotropic as it means to move toward a wholeness that embraces life beyond the ego and the body and identifies with cosmic consciousness. In this altered state, the psyche can bring significant events to our attention such as traumas, hidden sadness, guilt, or remorse in order to grieve, forgive or release powerful blocks to our well being. As Dr. Grof says, in the practice "We realize our own divinity and our essential deep connection with other people, nature, and all life."

Unlike weekly talk therapy with a psychiatrist or psychologist which can wade through years of life history, the issues with the most emotional relevance arise automatically in holotropic breathwork. Repressed physical or psychological traumas are brought to the surface quickly. One therapy is verbal while the other is experiential. Unlike talk therapy where experiences are just remembered, situations are actually *relived* in holotropic breathwork. Dr. Grof discovered that physical traumas can be the cause of a person's anxiety or depression, phobias, migraines, asthma or other maladies. Through reliving the harsh struggles, dramatic behavioral, emotional, and even physical improvements are made possible.

Why go to the trouble? Why is it so important to heal from psychic wounds? Certainly if one is in profound pain, they are going to seek relief to get back to being well. After all, the consequences of some wounds keep us from feeling loved, being kind, finding our voice, or feeling generous. As disease begins as a thought, healing begins by changing our thoughts at the soul level through understanding. And because we are connected to everything in the Universe, our own healing affects everyone and everything. Therefore, we contribute to the healing of the whole world by paying attention to our own curative work.

Without a physical wound, how can we know there is an underlying trauma, grief or distress? Sometimes we learn of soul distress if we have an unexplained phobia, an emotional instability, or an inability to cope. Some past experiences of shame, abandonment, or unworthiness might be so deeply repressed that we have effectively hidden them. A friend of mine was honestly perplexed by his constant anger so he entered holotropic breathwork as a way to unbury the cause. Being given the reason for powerful emotional blocks is like coming upon an oracle whose deity offers the seeker knowledge that was once concealed.

After signing up for a holotropic breathwork session, I watched all of the assigned training videos to ensure I would have a safe experience. After that due diligence, I felt both excited and a bit apprehensive as any moment in time could be relived. Would I return to the womb and experience being born, the last of three girls? Perhaps I'd hear Dad say he really wanted a boy. Or would I relive a time during the life of one of my ancestors, the one who was a horse thief, just when his karmic debt came due?

But this is what actually happened. Upon meeting our facilitator and the other adventurers, we shared an uplifting camaraderie. When we were comfortably lying on floor cushions with blankets to cover us, the beautiful, loud, music began and we breathed deeply and rapidly. Within minutes, I began trembling and got scared. However, I talked myself into embracing the constant shaking and the strong emotions the music provoked and felt courageous instead. Asking for another comforter helped, but I still seemed to be in an icy place, feeling as cold as the little girl I'd been pulling her sled up the hill on a snowy day in Minnesota.

.

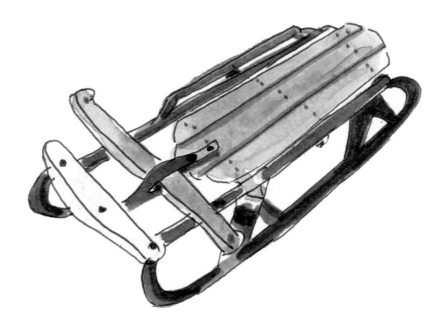

At first, I sensed the deep red colors associated with the base and sacral chakras and thought about a strong connection to a friend. As the energy rose to the solar plexus chakra, I came to believe I conceived my first child at that level and gave birth to him right then feeling a powerful adoration and enlivening unity with him. It felt as if he extended from my body. Then the Kundalini energy rose to my heart where I felt I conceived my second child and he extended from there. Again, I was flooded with a deep, abiding love and oneness with him. There were times throughout the session I felt like I was hearing the music he would compose.

Then after about an hour into the session, still breathing rapidly and deeply and surrounded by the evocative music. I felt vibrations in my upper body and a *vision* formed of a red-orange symmetrical cross filled with roses that were almost white. This was very significant to me as it was the same imagery written about by Rudolf Steiner and the Rosicrucians, the Brotherhood of the Rose Cross.

At the very center of the roses, I noticed something small and different so I zoomed in on that and the vision expanded to reveal hands clasping each other by the fingers. Later I learned this mudra, or hand position, is the Ganesha Mudra. Ganesha is the Hindu deity who overcomes obstacles and this mudra reportedly opens the fourth chakra, the heart, supplying courage, confidence, and openness to other people. During the whole three hour journey, I was very emotional, primarily because I felt ecstatic. But I also believe I was being forgiven for the guilt I carried regarding other people which lightened my burden during that larger time of personal malaise.

This was a successful soul healing for me and some of the others so I participated in several more sessions over a period of five years. In the breathwork following the death of my father, the music enveloped me to the point where I was able to grieve completely and honor his life. In another, I felt tremendous sorrow and guilt over the way I had judged and mistreated two important women in my life, both of whom had died. Because of the vibrations in my hands, I knew I could heal them and myself so I directed God's energy to us asking that our barriers to love be removed and I felt this happen. I spoke to them, was forgiven, and let them know how much I loved them. Their complete holiness became evident to me.

During another session, Scott, his fiancé, and Krishna were with me in a circle of light when all four of us joined hands in the sky. At the time, my son and his fiancé were in the Himalayas in Gangtok, Sikkim, and I had traveled through India the previous year. Circling in the sky above India, I felt the four of us were sending Divine healing to the country below us and we remained in this state for the next hour, my hands and feet constantly vibrating.

In another session, deity revealed to me that I had a physical, emotional, and mental block due to a specific loss from decades earlier. I began mourning that person's death with a grief I didn't realize I still harbored. Then I said aloud "My love for you is as deep as the ocean and as wide as the sea." Sensing a growing stream of light, I asked for one hundred angels to gather around me, which I believe happened. My grieving continued, but then I was prompted to think of all the individuals I knew, family, friends, and even former enemies, while I stated that same sentence "My love for you is as deep as the ocean and as wide as the sea" for each person separately. My heart opened up and my love expanded to become all inclusive. I realized then that I could love everyone, that we are all one, and in the words from A Course in Miracles, there truly are no 'special relationships.'

Through holotropic breathwork, I found a blessed modality of healing that was powerful and effective. It is not for the faint of heart and requires time, energy, honesty and courage. In such a transcendent experience, a person's vibration definitely speeds up and there is a lot of physical shaking. Healing in this altered state can be like an oracle, offering the gift of awareness, fresh understanding, forgiveness, release from past traumas, Divine love, and increased self compassion. Holotropic breathwork is one way to connect with our constructive healing power, a capacity to affect the world.

On and On

You must learn from the mistakes of others.
You can't possibly live long enough to make them all yourself.
Sam Levenson

Ah, but what if we *do* live long enough to make all the mistakes we possibly can? What if we have all the time in eternity to really Mess Up Big Time while playing on this peculiar planet? If you've remembered a past life, you're more likely to believe we experience life after life and that death is merely a door to another room in that mansion. There are times when I've just met a person and sense I already know them, or hear of a new place and feel an instant affinity for it or conversely perhaps, a strong aversion. Am I bumping up against a past life? Or a future life? There are pathways to finding out.

Some people have made it their life's work to interview children who remember their most recent past life and then document the validity of their recall. One was Ian Stevenson, a psychiatrist, who spent 40 years researching the children who spontaneously remembered their past life. He and his team investigated three thousand cases from around the world and verified many of them. Fortunately for me, I didn't even have to leave the neighborhood to find a child like that.

The daughter of my very close friend was just starting to talk in sentences when she began telling her mom about her previous life. In that life, she was an even younger child when "the kitchen was on fire. I was hiding under the table. My sister, (the same one she has now), picked me up and threw me out the window. I was caught by Jesus." She continued, "My mother was really bad. All the moms I've had were bad. You are the first good one." Fortunately, my friend listened to her daughter with an open mind, wrote down what she said, and gave her those notes - twenty years later.

Ian Stevenson found that people frequently maintain the same personality, facial features, and talents. However, they can be a different gender, race, or religious faith in another life. In one study Ian carried out on 31 sets of twins whose past-life identities were verified, he found that the twins had a past relationship as spouses, siblings or friends. (www.reincarnationresearch.com)

Another path to learning about past lives is in dreams. When I began recording my dreams, I programmed myself to wake up after *every one* so I wouldn't miss capturing the experience. However, I really got tired from waking up in the middle of every night so the experiment was short-lived. Nevertheless, I recorded two dreams that took place in the small hours of the night, around one o'clock, when past lives tend to appear in dreams. This was the first one.

> *I am walking beside my horse in the Ural Mountains which are covered in snow. My clothes are made of homespun, a coarsely woven fabric. I sense this life is over one thousand years ago.*

During my current life, I was intimidated by Russia. Growing up during the Cold War, the animosities between our countries were so treacherous I had nightmares of thermonuclear annihilation. Although I didn't have a clear sense of whether I was a man or woman in the Urals, my clothing was very primitive.

In my other dream of a past life, I was a girl in Europe, in about the 1300s and just as in the first one, I felt like I was actually there. As often happens in glimpses of a past life, the dream began when I was looking at my feet.

I am putting on black stockings, then black shoes followed by a black dress and white apron. I am a young woman, about sixteen, and am a maid in this prosperous house. The structure is partially built with large smooth stones and there is a full fire in the fireplace warming the room and lighting it up completely. I am a servant to a feudal nobleman who lives here. There is another maid and we are watching a couple of cats.

Once, I was in a group of about twelve seekers who gathered one evening with the intention of discovering our past lives. We sat on the floor in a circle in a darkened room taking turns holding a candle just below our face. For several minutes, everyone stared at the face in the candlelight with their eyes slightly squinted. Then the magic happened! The person's face transformed, including all the clothes around their face to reveal what they looked like and what they were wearing in a past life. *Even I* could see the switch! The most memorable sight for me was of a woman who became a man from hundreds of years ago wearing a luxurious red and gold Spanish cloak and a regal hat made of the same colorful fabrics.

When it was my turn in the candlelight, several people watched my face morph into that of a Viking man missing one eye. Unbeknownst to them, some of my ancestors are Norwegian. When I was a teenager, my father painted the likeness of a Viking stone carving done around 800 A.D. which I loved so much that I asked him for it, almost the only one of his paintings I ever requested.

Becoming aware of snippets from my past lives was enriching because it broadened my perspectives but I was unable to relate them to my current life. That's why I became so intrigued by the case of reincarnation of Barbro Karlen as she received so much information about her past over years and years.

Barbro was born in 1954 in Gothenburg, Sweden to a Christian couple and her recall to her previous life was spontaneous. When she began talking, she told her parents they were not her real parents and that her real name was Anne Frank. She gave them details from that life but her parents thought she was fantasizing. (Karlen, Barbro, *And the Wolves Howled*, Clairview Books, London 2000) At the time, they didn't know about the well known author because her book didn't become famous until after it was translated into German and English and the play "The Diary of Anne Frank" was written and performed in America.

Barbro had reoccurring nightmares of men in uniform running up stairs, kicking in the door, dogs barking, things being thrown about and having her precious red book being grabbed from her hands. In waking life, Barbro was terrified by people in uniforms, showers, and playing hide and seek. Kids chasing each other for fun petrified her. When Barbro was 7 or 8, her teacher began talking about Anne Frank which confused her because *she* was Anne Frank.

When she was ten, her parents took her to Amsterdam for the first time. Her parents wanted to visit the Anne Frank House so at their hotel, her father was ready to call for a taxi but Barbro told them they could walk there instead. She took them directly to the house, a ten minute walk from the hotel through convoluted streets. She noticed the steps to the house were different. (They had been rebuilt.) When she went inside, she became traumatized, like she did in her frequent nightmares. Upstairs in the annex where the Frank family hid, and while she was in Anne's bedroom, Barbro looked at the wall and briefly saw all of the pictures she had pinned up, even though her parents said nothing was there. The guide told them the pictures had just been removed temporarily to be put behind glass for protection. As she left her room, Barbro became so overcome with fear and grief, she told her mother she needed to leave right away and would wait for them outside. She collapsed at the bottom of the stairs, sobbing.

Although her father was annoyed by Barbro's behavior at Anne Frank's house, her mother believed her daughter, became convinced of reincarnation, and grew very spiritually minded. She was finally able to give her daughter the support she needed so their relationship became very close and Barbro was much happier. Eventually, her parents divorced.

Like Anne, Barbro was a prolific writer and was twelve when her first book was published. It became the best-selling book in Swedish history. By the time she was an adult, she had published nine books and those were translated into many languages. Similar to Anne, her writing was frequently about animals, nature, and harmony. From her personal experience, she wrote that "everyone was born again and again without exception." (Karlen, Barbro, *And the Wolves Howled*, Clairview Books, London 2000)

As she grew into her teens, the nightmares receded until Barbro thought she could put the whole trauma behind her. However, her life was a repeating pattern of victimization, of being bullied, and attacked. For many of her adult working years, two people tried to destroy her *relentlessly* through their persecution. She seems to suggest in her writing that the soldiers who persecuted her as Anne were in her life once again. The nightmares returned but they became more and more detailed showing her the connection between her lives.

Although she had a powerful experience of meeting the Christ as a girl, she only remembered to trust His love and care after suffering immeasurably as an adult. Through trust, miracles began to happen and she started to regain some peace. Finally, in her dreams, Barbro sat writing at Anne's desk in the hidden annex night after night and wrote down the same things in her journals during the day. Her fear from being in the annex and at the concentration camp diminished while she grew convinced that she deserved justice, that she had to stand up to her persecutors, and stop being a victim. Most importantly, the overlap in her lives taught her to forgive her tormentors.

In the space of only a couple of years, three of my friends told me about their flashbacks to another life, their most recent one. None of them knew each other but all three were academically bright women who had experienced anorexia when they were in their teens. In each case, the flashbacks were to being in a concentration camp. None of them were Jewish now but one seriously considered converting to Judaism.

For those who experience a past life, the awareness can be healing and empowering. Witnessing one or more lives testifies to the eternal nature of our souls. Past life recall broadens our perspective to the point where we are more compassionate to ourselves, more understanding of the people around us, and accepting of the roles we play in our lives.

Intentionally

I'm not crazy about reality, but it's still
the only place to get a decent meal.
Groucho Marx

It was just a glossy one page ad in a travel magazine. But it was the first time I ever saw a photo of a thatched roofed, over-the-water bungalow perched on stilts in a lagoon in the South Pacific. I fell in love. "Does such a place really exist" I wondered. My desire to fly to that cabana in the sun surrounded by a shallow, sheltered sea was immediate, firm and abiding. I would go there one day. The photo showed a little ladder descending from the deck into a sparkling turquoise ocean where I imagined snorkeling with brilliantly colored tropical fish. Unbeknownst to me, broadcasting that profound desire out to a loving Universe was like sending a sweet tweet into cyberspace that goes viral.

A few years later, I entered the local PBS TV member sweepstakes and won the Grand Prize – a week in the Tahitian islands for two! My husband and I were able to bring our young son, Scott, to live in those luxurious over-the-water bungalows. On the island of Bora Bora, we were awarded the cabana furthest from land. To get there, we walked on a wooden pier that meandered about the length of a football field out into the pristine lagoon. Even my travel averse husband was completely enchanted and asked me in a voice filled with awe, "Is this real?"

A rainstorm swept in one evening with a lovely, comforting patter on the thatch. As the walls rose up short of the roof, a refreshing breeze wafted over the partitions and through each room. When we were on land, lush tropical flowers dazzled us and perfumed the air. Coconut palms rustled quietly as they rose tall on the pure white sandy beaches and deep green plants covered the wild, rugged, iconic mountains of Bora Bora.

On the island of Moorea, we were given a bungalow that stood over the dolphin lagoon, especially delighting our son. As the three of us sat on our private deck, the dolphins jumped out of the water apparently for the sheer joy of leaping in front of their infatuated audience. They launched out of the water, climbed as high as possible, then gracefully arched over to dive in again. We heard them swim underneath our rooms at night and saw them pass below the glass coffee table in the living room during the day.

Entering the contest for the trip gave form to my intention, but I actually did something more. I demonstrated that desire by making changes to my house. While studying feng shui, the ancient Chinese art of using favorable spatial arrangements, I became familiar with the *bagua map*, a tool that ties areas in a house to success in relationships, career, knowledge, health, prosperity, and travel. This tool seemed to be a fascinating way to give form to intention. The location of the garage in my particular house corresponds to *travel and helpful people* on the map. Each house is different.

My garage needed a sturdy column to raise and support the sagging roof, so I rented a hydraulic lift to assist me. At the last minute, I had Ryan come into the garage to give me moral support and we succeeded in setting up a permanent, load bearing post together. I had no idea if anything would happen as a result of my changes as this was the first time I was aware of the relationships in feng shui. A couple of weeks later, Ryan won two airline tickets to Paris and he took me! After returning from the beguiling City of Light, I made additional improvements to the garage by organizing, cleaning it, and painting the floor. Shortly after that, I won the trip to the islands of Tahiti.

Winning those trips bolstered my conviction something superb would happen when I made changes to our sunroom. My recognition of the true nature of a loving Universe was growing. According to the bagua map, the sunroom in our house corresponds to *children and creativity*. I re-carpeted the room in a bright new color and rearranged all the furniture. At the time, Scott was in the fifth grade at a nearby Waldorf school. Within a couple of weeks, I was called to accept the lead in the school's production of "Amahl and the Night Visitors." The project also had me creating costumes for the many children in the opera. Scott played the role of my son which gave us the opportunity to sing and act together on stage. It became my fondest memory from his many years at the school.

It is written in the Bible that thought and belief can combine to create power to move mountains. Is it arrogant to believe we have such power? Jesus says in A Course in Miracles "Who assumes a power that he does not possess is deceiving himself. Yet to accept the power given him by God is but to acknowledge his Creator and accept His gifts." (M-29.5). Although we often prefer to believe our private thoughts can't possibly have any influence, there are no idle thoughts. They always have an effect, even if we aren't conscious of it.

When I was a brand new student of this power, I enthusiastically shared what I'd learned with my brother in law, Wes. He was so skeptical of that potential, he challenged me saying "Well, if that's true, then have Chairman Chernenko tell the world he wants to end the cold war, change the relationship between our countries to one of peaceful coexistence, and work with us to stop the nuclear arms race." That night, I decided to take Wes up on his challenge and directed my thoughts to that end. Within a couple of weeks, I read in the newspaper Chernenko announced that the first priority in Soviet-American relations was "the limitation and reduction of arms, and above all nuclear arms…look not to confrontation but to peaceful coexistence." (announced Nov. 17, 1984.) I was so taken aback, I didn't even tell Wes.

It appears miracles find size irrelevant. Growing up in Minnesota, I was accustomed to dramatic weather like blinding snowstorms, gigantic thunderclouds, pelting hail, deafening lighting strikes, and ominous tornado sirens. But in 1961, when I watched and heard a TV anchor report on a hurricane while broadcasting from the site of Carla's landfall in Galveston, I knew I wanted to be in one of those, too. The anchor made it seem so thrilling. It didn't hurt that the reporter was young, dark, and handsome with a deep, rich voice, one that caught the attention of CBS News who later hired him. Ultimately, Dan Rather became a household name due to Hurricane Carla.

It also appears miracles find time as irrelevant as size. As you know, Minnesota is a wee bit short on hurricanes. But fourteen years after that newscast, I was living in Ft. Walton Beach, Florida when the eye of hurricane Eloise passed right through nearby Panama City. Earlier, my husband and other pilots from Hurlburt Field and Eglin AFB evacuated planes to inland states. As the daylight sky grew dark, my house guests and I stocked up on food and taped X's on the windows to keep the glass from shattering. A friend, who had to evacuate his beach cottage, took refuge in my house adding one more to our party. After keeping vigil all night due to the roaring frenzy of the wind and rain, we watched the trees bend in the light of dawn then break as water rose in the street. A little later, I drove a mile to the Gulf of Mexico and walked on the beach, thrilled by the roiling skies, angry wind, and waves crashing with a height and intensity I'd never seen before.

There are much more common situations where I use intention for desired weather outcomes. For instance, when I fly commercially and encounter turbulence, I visualize the air in front of the plane lying down to become a smooth road for miles and miles ahead. This seems to work consistently. Another situation is holding off rain. At the afternoon garden wedding of my nephew, rain was imminent so my sister Jean and I agreed to use the power of mind to repeat a reassuring answer to guests' concerns. "No! It won't rain until we're all inside for dinner." I'm sure they thought we had the local meteorologist on speed dial. This spoken denial held it off. All the guests were barely inside for dinner when the sky opened up and it rained cats and dogs.

When we were girls, Jean, and I auditioned for the high school musicals. During those times when my self confidence flagged, she became my cheerleader, encouraging me with her words which gave me the confidence to perform my best to secure a lead. Similarly, during my training to become a scuba diver, my instructor used pep talk because every skill I needed to learn was exceedingly difficult. "You can do this!" he emphatically stated so often that his assurance propelled me through the entire process to become certified.

We constantly create our immediate world and our personal future through our intentions. These are built out of strong desire from whatever inspires us. Depending on the strength of that desire, the power of our thoughts, the demonstration of our goal, or the use of denials or affirmations, we are graced with a loving response from the Universe when its power flows to and through us. No matter the size, no matter the timing, thoughts and feelings set the creative process in motion. Supernatural grace showers us with surprising, loving gifts - visions, uplifting dreams, strength in times of peril, illuminating truths, synchronicities, rain at the right time, smoother flights, right relationships, dramatic experiences, creative opportunities, and inspiring travels.

Published in Unity Magazine

Chapter One
Spirit Animals first appeared in Unity Magazine
September/October 2017 issue as "Groundhog Guru."

Chapter Two
Creating the Experience first appeared in Unity Magazine
July/August 2018.

Chapter Four
Flashes of the Future first appeared in Unity Magazine
March/April 2019.

Chapter Five
Accidentally Speaking first appeared in Unity Magazine
July/August 2020.

Chapter Six
Entangled first appeared in Unity Magazine
September/October 2018.

Chapter Eight
Sacred Serpent first appeared in Unity Magazine
September/October 2020.

Chapter Ten
The Healing Art of Breathwork was accepted for publication.

Acknowledgements

I thank the editor of Unity Magazine, Katy Koontz, for her generous time, enthusiastic praise, and work revising six of the book's chapters. I am indebted to Susan Lendvay, former Editor of Venture Inward, along with Jennie Taylor Martin and Alison Ray of the A.R.E. for their heartfelt encouragement as the articles took shape. I am immensely grateful to Kristi Townsend and Susan Lendvay for their steady, exuberant feedback. Scott Jespersen edited several stories for which I am very grateful.

Recommended Reading

A Course in Miracles, workbook, and text
Journey Beyond Words, Brent Haskell Ph.D.
Forgiveness and Jesus, Kenneth Wapnick Ph.D.
The Disappearance of the Universe, Gary R. Renard
There is a River, Thomas Sugrue
Many Mansions, Gina Cerminara
And There Was Light, Jacques Lusseyran
Expecting Adam, Martha Beck
The Power of Now, Eckhart Tolle
A New Earth, Eckhart Tolle
The Way of the Peaceful Warrior, Dan Millman
The Alchemy of Sacred Living, Emory J. Michael
The Holographic Universe, Michael Talbot
As a Man Thinketh, James Allen
Think and Grow Rich, Napolean Hill
Autobiography of a Yogi, Paramahansa Yogananda
You Can Heal Your Life, Louise Hay
The Essential Steiner, Robert A. McDermott
Be Love Now, Ram Dass
The Key to Yourself, Dr. V. Bloodworth
Power of Positive Thinking, Dr. Norman Vincent Peale
Life After Life, Raymond Moody M.D.
Zen and the Art of Motorcycle Maintenance, Robert M. Pirsig
Creative Visualization, Shakti Gawain
The Road Less Traveled, M. Scott Peck M.D.
Black Elk Speaks, Black Elk
The Varieties of Religious Experience, William James

Made in the USA
Middletown, DE
20 June 2021